FOLLOWING GOD'S COMPASS

Margaret Cherry

WESTBOW
PRESS®
A DIVISION OF THOMAS NELSON
& ZONDERVAN

WestBow Press books may be ordered through booksellers or by contacting:

WestBow Press
A Division of Thomas Nelson & Zondervan
1663 Liberty Drive
Bloomington, IN 47403
www.westbowpress.com
844-714-3454

ISBN: 979-8-3850-3058-3 (sc)
ISBN: 979-8-3850-3059-0 (e)

Library of Congress Control Number: 2024916130

Print information available on the last page.

WestBow Press rev. date: 08/14/2024

CONTENTS

A PERSONAL NOTE

It's hard for me to remember a time when God was not real to me. Looking back, I can see God's hand in my life's journey as a Christian. My wonderful older sister, Merlene, started taking me to Sunday School when I was about seven years old. When I was about twelve years old, I became a Christian and was baptized. I went to church regularly but I was in my twenties before I realized I had never let Jesus be Lord of my life, only my Savior. After that, my relationship with Jesus took on new meaning.

God gave us a compass to guide us through life so we would not be lost. God's compass is the Holy Bible, His Word, whose truths are revealed to us through His Holy Spirit. If we keep our eyes and heart on His compass, He will lead us on the right path.

King David wrote in Psalm119:105: *"Your word is a lamp for my feet, a light on my path."* And in John 16:13-14, Jesus said: *"But when He, the Spirit of truth, comes, He will guide you into all truth. He will not speak on His own; He will speak only what He hears, and He will tell you what is yet to come. He will bring glory to me by taking from what is mine and making it known to you."*

I wish I could say that I was always faithful, but I made many foolish mistakes. God's Holy Spirit was always there to help me get back on the right path. Over the years, there have been good times, bad times, and worse times, but Jesus has always given me strength for the day.

There were times when the circumstances of my life didn't change, but God gave me hope and strength to get me through them. He was there when my daughter was dying and showed me a miracle of healing. He was there when my husband got cancer that resulted in a heart attack, stroke, and the loss of a leg. He was there when my husband became ill with a life-threatening disease that required daily care. God sustained him for thirty years before He took him home to heaven.

I am blessed to have been a Christian for most of my life. It has been quite a journey! I do not pretend to be wise or to be a great Christian. I am just so grateful for all the ways God has revealed to me His grace, unfathomable compassion, forgiveness, strength and love at the times I have needed it so much. I feel that I should share this with others and praise God for showing it to me. My prayer is that in some small way it will bring a blessing and comfort to someone else, and will introduce Jesus to someone who doesn't know Him.

You may have many people who love you but remember, NOBODY LOVES YOU LIKE JESUS DOES. Let Him in your heart and life today.

Margaret Cherry

DEDICATION

Floyd

This book is dedicated to Floyd Edward Cherry, my late husband of 59 years, and my best friend. To paraphrase singer, songwriter Alan Jackson, "He was a true southern gentleman and he stood for our Flag and knelt to Jesus." I wrote this elegy for him.

We stood at the altar so many years ago
And vowed to love each other, all others to forego.
Together our lives began, Jesus, you and me.

Time went by, the babies came. We made a home and became a family.
There was joy, but also tears, as we learned to live in harmony.
Now our children joined Jesus, you and me.

Our Autumn years slipped up on us. Today our Lord called you home.
There was no fear in your eyes for you were not alone.
I feel us here together, Jesus, you and me.

I'm sure you know that I love you so. That will always be true.
I will be able to carry on for I'll have with me a part of you.
We'll still be here together, Jesus, you and me.

Your strength, your tenderness, your love, the way you liked to hold
my hand
Will help me face the lonely times, lift my spirits and help me stand.
As I feel us here together, Jesus, you and me.

Never would I wish you back, for Heaven must be far more grand.
There is no pain or heartache there, for in God's presence you will stand
Together with Jesus, and be free.

Watch for me. Watch for me. I'll not be far behind.
Listen; for I will call to you, and one sweet day you'll find
We'll all be there together, Jesus, you and me.

We'll sit by the Crystal Sea singing and praising the God we love.
What rejoicing there will be that day when we finally meet in Glory
above.
We'll share our lives forever, Jesus, you and me.

THE LOVE
CHAPTER

Chapter 13 of 1st Corinthians in the Bible has come to be known as the "Love Chapter". The last verse of that chapter is familiar to almost everyone, even to people who have not read the whole Bible. The message in that verse applies to all of us.

"And now these three remain: faith, hope and love. But the greatest of these is love." 1st Corinthians 13:13

One reason love is greatest is because it will continue, even grow throughout eternity. When we believers are in heaven, faith and hope will have fulfilled their purpose. We won't need faith because we will see God face to face and know that He is all that He said He is. We won't need hope in the second-coming of Jesus once He comes. But we will always love the Lord and each other, and that love will grow forever and ever.

Another reason love is the greatest is because it is an attribute of God. In 1st John 4:8, we are told: *"Whoever does not love does not know God, because God is love."* Faith and hope are not necessarily a part of God's character. God does not have faith in the way we have faith, because He never has to trust outside of himself. God does not have hope in the way we have hope, because He knows all things and is in complete control. But GOD IS LOVE, and will always be love.

The apostle wrote to Christians in Romans 8:38-39: *"For I am convinced that neither death nor life, neither angels nor demons, neither the present nor the future, nor any powers, neither height nor depth, nor anything else in all creation, will be able to separate us from the love of God that is in Christ Jesus our Lord."*

Nobody loves you like Jesus does.
Let Him in your heart today.
Nobody loves you like Jesus does.
Please don't turn Him away,

He knows when you're happy and when you're blue.
He hears you when you pray.
He takes away your sin and makes all things new.
Please don't turn Him away.

He burns the sun and He lights the stars.
He made the Milky Way.
You can come to Him just the way you are.
Please don't turn Him away.

Wandering along in fear and pain, my life in disarray.
Tired and alone with no hope in sight, I had lost my way.
Then Jesus came and took my pain. He held out His hand to me.
Since Jesus came, I am not the same. He saved me and set me free.

Nobody loves me like Jesus does.
He came into my heart that day.
Nobody loves me like Jesus does.
I couldn't turn Him away.

He loves us so much His blood He shed
When He hung on the cross that day.
Evil was defeated when He rose from the dead.
Please don't turn Him away.

Nobody loves you like Jesus does.
Let Him in your heart today.

Nobody loves you like Jesus does.
Please don't turn Him away.

"For God so loved the world that He gave His one and only son, that whoever believes in Him should not perish but have eternal life." John 3:16

"But God demonstrates his own love for us in this: while we were still sinners, Christ died for us." Romans 5:8

"...how shall we escape if we ignore such a great salvation?" Hebrews 2:3

GUARDING
OUR SPEECH

"Do not go about spreading slander among your people." Leviticus 19:16

"Lord, who may dwell in your sanctuary? Who may live on your holy hill? He whose walk is blameless, and who does what is righteous, who speaks the truth from his heart and has no slander on his tongue, who does his neighbor no wrong, and cast no slur on his fellowman." Psalm 15: 1-3

"Do not let any unwholesome talk come out of your mouths, but only what is helpful for building others up according to their needs, that it may benefit those who listen." Ephesians 4:29

"Without wood a fire goes out; without gossip a quarrel dies down." Proverbs 26:20

"A perverse man stirs up dissension, and a gossip separates close friends." Proverbs 16:28

"Consider what a great forest is set on fire by a small spark. The tongue also is a fire, a world of evil among the parts of the body. It corrupts the whole person, sets the whole course of his life on fire, and is itself set on fire by hell. All kinds of animals, birds, reptiles and creatures of the sea are being tamed and have been tamed by man, but no man can tame the tongue. It is a restless evil, full of deadly poison. With the tongue we praise our Lord and Father, and with it we curse

men, who have been made in God's likeness. Out of the same mouth come praise and cursing. My brother, this should not be." James 3:5-10

Jesus tells us in Matthew 12:36-37: *"But I tell you that man will have to give account on the day of judgment for every careless word they have spoken. For by your words, you will be acquitted, and by your words you will be condemned."* SCARY, ISN'T IT!

There is little to be added to what God has told us about how we should or shouldn't use our speech, except to say: **"Be careful what you say."** We are all guilty of gossip, lying, hurtful and unwholesome talk. If we think not, we fool ourselves. We should remember to think before we speak. May God help us to use our speech for His glory.

"Be kind and compassionate to one another, forgiving each other, just as in Christ God forgave you." Ephesians 4:32

"Don't grumble against each other, brother, or you will be judged. THE JUDGE IS STANDING AT THE DOOR." James 5:9

WHEN THE
STORMS COME

My husband, Floyd, was born about 150 years too late. He would have enjoyed being a wilderness man. From the time he was a young boy, he enjoyed camping and hunting and fishing. This love of the outdoors lasted throughout his adult years until poor health kept him from getting out. He had many adventures and he loved telling them to anyone who would sit and listen.

One night he was camping with two other men. It was a warm, clear night without a cloud in the sky. They set up camp and were sitting around the campfire telling hunting stories. They noticed that there was one small dark cloud moving slowly in their direction. They continued to talk and were not paying attention to the sky, when suddenly the cloud was over them. It was only a few feet wide but it started to rain on them, heavy enough to put out their fire and soak everything in the camp, especially them. Then, just as quickly as it came, it moved on.

Have you ever had a time in your life when it seemed that you had a cloud that followed you around and rained on you continually? I have felt that way. It seemed that my life was just one crisis after another and that the sun would never shine again for me. But I learned many things while in those stormy times. The most amazing truth that I discovered is that I felt the presence of God's Spirit closer to me than at any other time. I found that when I was too weak to go on, I could. Not by my strength but by the power of the Holy Spirit that lived within me.

I must admit that there still are times when I feel alone and angry and I have an occasional meltdown. But when I turn it over to Jesus, He gives me a peace that I cannot explain. The things that I am dealing with may not always change; sometimes God has to change me.

"God, the eternal God, is our support at all times, especially when we are sinking into deep trouble. There are seasons when we sink quite low...Dear child of God, even when you are at your lowest, underneath are the everlasting arms." Charles Spurgeon

"...because God has said, 'Never will I leave you, never will I forsake you', so we say with confidence; 'The Lord is my helper, I will not be afraid. What can man do to me'." Hebrews 13:5,6

"...The Lord is near; do not be anxious about anything, but in everything, by prayer and petition, with thanksgiving, present your requests to God. And the peace of God, which transcends all understanding, will guard your hearts and your minds in Christ Jesus." Philippians 4:5-7

"I have told you these things so that in me you may have peace. In this world you will have trouble. But take heart! I have overcome the world." John 16:33

GOD WILL GO WITH YOU

God will go with you; He will not forsake you.
The battles you face will be His battles too.
Where He leads you, He's been there before you.
Jesus has said it and His words are true.

Over the mountain and through the dark valley,
He'll guide your pathway with the light of His love
He will not fail you. You have only to trust Him.
When the pathway gets rocky, just look above.

When Satan whispers "You can go no further"
And your heart is weary and doubt comes to call,
Remember how Peter walked on that water;
While he focused on Jesus, he did not fall.

Jesus will go with you all the way home.
He will go with you to the end of the road.
He will never change and He will never roam.
When your burden is heavy, He'll carry your load.

God's strength is perfect when we are the weakest.
He will give you peace when those evil days come.
When your race is run and your journey's complete,
Jesus will come in His glory to take you home.

TODAY IS MY BIRTHDAY

Today is my birthday. But instead of celebrating it as my special day, I would like to honor my mother who gave so much to me and my brothers and sisters. My father left me and five other siblings when I was twelve years old. Being our mother meant that she seldom had a new dress, never went out to eat, never had a new car, got out of bed before daylight to be at a job before the sun came up, seldom got to attend our school functions, and had to depend on us to look after each other most of the time. She sometimes worked two jobs to pay the bills. She seldom hugged us or told us that she loved us, but we always felt loved. She said "I love you" everyday by the sacrifices she made and the things that she did for us.

Do we only spend time with our mother on her birthday and Mother's Day and maybe give her a call now and then? If it is possible to do so, maybe those of us who are blessed to still have our mother here, should spend more time with her. That precious one-on-one time I spent with my mother before God called her home is one of my most treasured memories. God commands us to honor and respect our mother. Those of us who were blessed with loving mothers should do it willingly and with loving gratitude.

This is my tribute to my mother. Hope you will see some of your mother's qualities in these words.

MY MAMA

Mama had green eyes—but not green like you think.
Her Irish eyes sparkled when she smiled with a playful wink.
She was a pretty woman and was so until the day she died.
Not beautiful, but pretty, pretty that comes from the inside.

Mama was raised on a truck farm—working hard was her fate,
For she had seven children by the time she was twenty-eight.
She never finished school; she got married when she was just a kid.
So, she wanted us to finish school and made sure that we all did.

She could milk a cow, skin a hog, pluck a chicken, and shoot a rifle too.
While growing up I believed there was nothing she couldn't do.
She taught me how to fish, make jelly, cook, and sew my own clothes.
I learned how to plant a garden, can the vegetables, and how to plant a rose.

Daddy was a mechanic, so Mama never had a car that was new.
We always had an old car that he kept running, and she just had to
make do.
We never seemed to live in a house that wasn't old or way too small.
We shared clothes, rooms and beds, and the furniture was always
wall-to-wall.

But somehow Mama made wherever we lived into a welcome place.
Making a house a home is more than décor, furnishings, and space.
There was laughter, sharing, arguing, discipline and fun—lots of fun.
Mama was the loving bond that held us together, after all was said and done.

We were rich in things that count, though to the world we looked poor.
Thanks to Mama, we felt loved, accepted and proud; who could ask
for more?
We knew that we were not just clothed and fed, but were cherished
and loved,
And that we were lifted up in prayer and placed in the hands of God
above.

When we all grew up and she was alone and I had more time with her to spend,

She became more that just my mother; I found in her a trusted friend.

I'm thankful that God blessed me with this Christian mother who came to be

The mother who loved me, guided me, taught me, and allowed me to be me.

"God can't be everywhere so He created mothers." I read that somewhere.

I know that God can be everywhere but this is a sweet sentiment I like to share.

When I consider the amazing grace of God and the great love that is His,

And then I consider the love of a godly mother, maybe her love is second only to His.

"She speaks with wisdom, and faithful instruction is on her tongue. She watches over the affairs of her household and does not eat the bread of idleness. Her children arise and call her blessed..." Proverbs 31:26-28

"Honor your father and your mother, so that you may live long in the land the Lord your God is giving you." Exodus 20:12

DO YOU BELIEVE
IN MIRACLES?

I once read about a Christian college student who became engaged in a debate with an agnostic professor about the validity of the Bible's recording of miracles. The professor did not believe in miracles; he believed that everything can be logically explained or proven by science. In the course of the exchange between them, the professor tried to explain away the crossing of the Red Sea by the Israelites when they were fleeing with Moses from the Egyptian army. The professor pointed out that probably some of the bottom of the Red Sea is rock. His explanation to his class was that there may have been sections of the Red Sea that were shallow, some sections being only a few inches deep. So, the Israelites would have been able to cross the sea in safety.

The college student paused a moment and then replied to the professor: "If the Israelites were able to cross the Red Sea in safety, the real miracle is that the entire Egyptian army, including the horses, drowned in just a few inches of water!"

A lot of time and effort is spent by unbelievers trying to explain away the miracles that are recorded in the Bible, as well as the miracles that still occur every day. People tend to ignore or pass off as coincidence, fate or luck the stories of miracles in our everyday life. My daughter's life was spared through the power of prayer by a merciful and compassionate God. What a humbling experience! I have found that whenever I try to tell people about her miraculous healing, they tend to change the subject or just act bored or disinterested. I get the feeling that they just humor me or think of me as one of those fanatical religious people or that they just don't believe me.

Have we become so blasé and sophisticated in our thinking that it is becoming impossible to believe in the miracles that God performs every day? Judging from the popular television shows about half-dead zombies and supernatural beings, it would seem that there is an interest in the after-life. Then, why is it so hard for some people to believe in Jesus, the only one who has ever conquered death and risen from the grave to walk among his followers?

Jesus warned: *"In them is fulfilled the prophecy of Isaiah: 'You will be ever hearing but never understanding; you will be ever seeing but never perceiving. For this people's heart has become calloused; they hardly hear with their ears, and they have closed their eyes. Otherwise, they might see with their eyes, and hear with their ears, understand with their hearts and turn, and I would heal them.'"* Matthew 13:14-15

"He is not here; HE IS RISEN!" Luke 24:6

THE WELCOMING
ARMS OF JESUS

If we are honest with ourselves, we all might confess that death, with its mysterious unknown, causes us some apprehension—even those of us who know where we are going when we die. Jesus had no fear of death. He had power over the final enemy. While on earth, He raised many from the dead and willingly invited His own death so you and I could be redeemed and made righteous before His heavenly Father.

Most of us have experienced the grief of losing someone we loved very much. Even if we know they are with Jesus, we miss them and long to see them again. I like to think of the passing of a dear one as described in the following anonymous story.

I am standing upon the seashore. A ship at my side spreads her white sails to the morning breeze and starts for the blue ocean. She is an object of beauty and strength, and I stand and watch her until at length she hangs like a speck of white cloud just where the sea and sky come down to mingle with each other. Then someone at my side says: "There! She's gone."

Gone where? Gone from my sight—that is all. She is just as large in mast and hull and spar as she was when she left my side, and just as able to bear her load of living freight to the place of destination. Her diminished size is in me, not in her. As she disappears from my sight she is welcomed by other eyes on the other shore. They watch her grow larger as she gets closer to the shore; and just at the moment when someone says, "There! She's gone," other voices take up the glad shout, "Look! Here she comes!"

What a comfort to know that as our loved ones pass from our sight, they are welcomed into the arms of Jesus who waits on the other shore.

Jesus prayed: *"Father, I want those you have given me to be with me where I am, and to see my glory, the glory you have given me because you loved me before the creation of the world."* John 17:24

"Do not let your hearts be troubled. Trust in God, trust also in me. In my Father's house are many rooms; if it were not so, I would have told you. I am going there to prepare a place for you. And if I go and prepare a place for you, I will come back and take you to be with me that you also may be where I am." John 14:1-3

PICTURE ME THERE

One day when God has called me home
You may shed a tear.
But where I am you can come,
If you trust our Lord so dear.

When you feel sad because I'm not there,
Will you do one thing for me?
Just picture me there in heaven so fair
With God, and angels as far as you can see.

Sitting on the shore beside the Crystal Sea,
Resting under the shade of a flowering tree,
Feeling a gentle breeze--that is where I will be
Waiting for you to come and share forever with me.

Think of me there in His presence--the One who gave us life;
With no more worries, no more pain, no more earthly strife.
In that beautiful land filled with peace and serenity,
Someday you and I will be together there for all eternity.

BE A BLESSING

I was just eighteen years old when my father-in-law died. He had been gravely ill for some time and my mother-in-law had cared for him at home. They had lived in town for many years and, being a small town, almost everyone in town knew the family. The days before the funeral were filled with people in and out of their home, bringing food or just stopping by to offer their condolences. At times there was a crowd and it was all a bit overwhelming.

My mother-in-law had a saintly friend, Mrs. Brown, who came early every day to their house and took over the kitchen. She made sure the dishes were washed, the coffee pot was full, and that the family was fed. Whenever visitors would come, she answered the door, offered them refreshments, and cleaned up when they left. My mother-in-law was free to sit down and visit with her guests.

I don't remember much about the funeral service, such as who conducted the service or who sang or if there were any testimonials, but I have never forgotten what Mrs. Brown did. She made a very difficult time much easier on a grieving family. She showed her love in the best way she knew how by fulfilling a need, quietly and practically unnoticed. Even though I was just eighteen, she made a lasting impression on me.

"The people who influence us the most are not those who buttonhole us and talk to us, but those who live their lives like the stars in heaven and the lilies of the field, perfectly simple and unaffectedly. Those are the lives that mold us. If you want to be of use to God, get rightly related to Jesus Christ and He will make you of use unconsciously every minute you live." Oswald Chambers

"Do not shine so that others may see you; shine so that through you, others may see Him." C. S. Lewis

"Therefore, as we have opportunity, let us do good to all people, especially to those who belong to the family of believers." Galatians 6:10

"Offer hospitality to one another without grumbling. Each one should use whatever gift he has received to serve others, faithfully administering God's grace in its various forms. If anyone speaks, he should do it as one speaking the very words of God. If anyone serves, he should do it with the strength God provides, so that in all things God may be praised through Jesus Christ. To him be the glory and the power for ever and ever. Amen" 1 Peter 4:9-11

When angels come to visit us, they are sent by God above.
This is just one way our Heavenly Father sends to us His love.
Quietly, unnoticed, they help us bear our trouble and our sorrow;
By God's grace, giving strength for today and hope for tomorrow.

We may not see their gossamer wings or halos so bright and grand;
But God's love shines in their eyes and His strength is in their hands.
They tenderly give the touch of love as they so sweetly serve our needs.
"God loves you" is said so clearly by their presence and their deeds.

Angels need not fly around in white robes with halos bright and shiny;
They may look ordinary—some tall, some short, some big, some tiny.
They may just give a hug, a kind word, a smile, or just say "I love you."
So, when you feel God so near, do not always look above you.

Did an angel come to you today and help God show His love to you?
Did you recognize that He was there to help you make it through?
Are you willing to accept His love and share it with a sister or a brother?
You may be the angel God will use to say "I love you" to another.

WHAT IS GOD LIKE?

Knowing about God is not the same as knowing God. Through the words and life of Jesus we can see who God is and what he is like. In John 14:9, Jesus told his disciples, *"Anyone who has seen me has seen the Father."* To see what God is like, we must look at Jesus.

First of all, Jesus was born into an ordinary home and family. Jesus' humble birth identified with human birth, ordinary folks, and childhood forever. He knows all the challenges of living together in an ordinary home and in a big family.

Jesus was a hard-working carpenter. He knows the difficulty of making a living. He no-doubt had to deal with ill-mannered customers and the client who will not pay his bill. He faced the problems with which we have to deal in the workplace, in our family life, and our finances. He knows what it is like to work hard and be tired at the end of the day. He knows the satisfaction that comes when a task is completed and well-done.

Jesus knows what it is like to be misunderstood and unappreciated. In His Word, He shows us the everyday struggles He had to go through and how to have victory over those struggles. He knows first-hand what it is like to be mistreated, and to face the daily worldly temptations that surround us.

In Jesus we see a loving God. The moment love enters our life it brings pain along with it. If we could be free and detached from caring for anything and anyone, we could be free from pain and human sorrow. In Jesus, we see God caring for His children, loving them beyond measure. Because of this incomprehensible love, He can say to us that we must love him and love one another as He loves us.

Last of all, we see Jesus on a cross. This is so incredible. It is easy to imagine a God who condemns men, one who could wipe out men who oppose him. No one would ever have dreamed of a God who, in Jesus Christ, chose the cross to die for us and our redemption. Jesus is the revelation of God, and that revelation should leave us humbled and amazed, and filled with wonder, love, and praise.

"You see, at just the right time, when we were powerless, Christ died for the ungodly. Very rarely will anyone die for a righteous man, though for a good man someone might possibly dare to die. But God demonstrates his love for us in this: while we were still sinners, Christ died for us." Romans 5:6-8

Jesus said: **"I am the way and the truth and the life. No one comes to the Father except through me.** *If you really knew me, you would know my Father as well. From now on, you do know him and have seen Him."* John 14:6-7

Sin had taken me over with such a strong hold,
I couldn't see any way to get back my soul.
With His precious blood, Jesus covered my sin;
Forgave me and made me whole once again.
How can I not love a Savior like that?

I often stumble and many times I fall down.
It's then that He picks me up and turns me around.
Sometimes I wander but when I humbly pray,
He takes my hand and helps me find my way.
How can I not love a Savior like that?

Because of His compassion and His great love,
He left His heavenly throne in Glory above.
He was born in the shadow of Calvary's cross.
He came to redeem me-one so hopelessly lost.
How can I not love a Savior like that?

He has now returned to His heavenly home,
But He did not forsake me or leave me alone.
He sent His Holy Spirit to live in my heart;
And though I can't see Him, we are never apart.
How can I not love a Savior like that?

"We will never see such a miracle again; God in His great love came to us as a man!" Anonymous

SNAKE IN
THE GRASS

Recently there was a documentary on PBS about the invasion of the Burmese python into the Everglades National Park in south Florida. According to this program, there is an estimated 150,000 pythons in the park and the number is growing. These snakes can grow to be very large and they have no natural enemies in this environment. There are countless other alien species there and together with the snakes, they are destroying the natural habitat at an alarming rate. Some authorities say there is no way to eradicate them, only to keep them under control. Others are more pessimistic; they think the problem has been ignored too long and that nothing can be done to reverse the damage.

These snakes are consuming the animals and birds as well as what they feed on to survive. The only creatures they cannot kill and eat are the really large alligators and native crocodiles. However, as the documentary pointed out, there are very few of these creatures and their young are being preyed upon every day.

Once there was another natural garden spot that was invaded by a snake and was ultimately uninhabitable by man---the Garden of Eden. The snake that was able to slither his way in was Satan himself. And, like the Burmese python, ever since that day he has been attacking mankind and his offspring, and has been taking over as much of God's creation as he can. But Satan has someone who is more powerful than him—the omnipotent God who created the world he is trying to destroy.

Unlike the creatures who are helpless to overcome the attack of the Burmese pythons, we are not without a protector. Jesus Christ, the beloved Son of God, came from his throne in heaven to live among us and show us the face of God. He suffered and died on a Roman cross to be the ultimate sacrifice for our sins, so that we might be acceptable to our Father in heaven. When we come to him and confess our sins and repent and ask for his forgiveness, He forgives us and receives us into his kingdom. He does not forsake us or leave us to fight our earthly and spiritual battles with Satan alone. He empowers us with His Holy Spirit and with his help, we can overcome.

"Who shall separate us from the love of Christ? Shall trouble or hardship or persecution or famine or nakedness or danger or sword? As it is written: 'For your sake we face death all day long; we are considered as sheep to be slaughtered.' No, in all things we are more than conquerors through him who loved us. For I am convinced that neither death nor life, neither angels nor demons, neither the present nor the future, nor any powers, neither height nor depth, nor anything else in all creation, will be able to separate us from the love of God that is in Christ Jesus our Lord." Romans 8:35-39

"What, then, shall we say in response to this? If God be for us, who can be against us?" Romans 8:31

HOW NOT TO PRAY

During Jesus' days on earth, there was hardly an occasion in the life of a devout Jew that didn't have a stated formula for prayer. It was the intention that every happening in life should be brought into the presence of God. The devout Jew had set times for prayer and wherever they might be at those times they were required to pray. Some of them would be certain to be in a conspicuous public place at those times to pray, so that they would appear pious. Often, their prayers would be long and composed to impress those around them rather than being addressed to God.

Jesus condemned this practice in Matthew 6:5-6 when He said: *"And when you pray, you must not be like the hypocrites, for they are fond of praying standing in the synagogues and at the corners of the streets, so that they may be seen by people. This is the truth I tell you—they are paid in full. But when you pray, go into your private room, and shut the door, and pray to your Father who is in secret; and your Father who sees what happens in secret will give you your reward in full."*

Jesus said, *"When you pray, do not pile up meaningless phrases, as the Gentiles do, for their idea is that they will be heard because of the length of their words. So, then, do not be like them, for your Father knows the things you need before you ask him."* Matthew 6:7-8

Jesus gave us two great rules for prayer. First: He said that all true prayer must be offered to God and not the people around us who are listening. When we pray, whether in private or public, our thoughts and desires should be addressed to God as we humble ourselves before Him. Second: we must remember that God is a loving God and is more ready to answer than we are to pray. It isn't necessary to coax, pester, or bargain in order to receive an answer from God. If we can remember this, we will be able to go to God with our prayers and sincerely pray, *"Thy will be done."*

Jesus continues to tell us how to pray in Matthew 6:9-13, by giving us what has come to be identified as "The Lord's Prayer". If we want a personal relationship with Jesus, we must humble ourselves and talk to Him. Prayer is communion with God. What a baffling but glorious privilege it is for us, common and sinful as we are, to be able to approach the throne of Almighty God.

In the precious name of Jesus, I offer up this prayer
To my Savior who has loved me and kept me in His care.
I thank Him for His blessings as I walk from day to day;
As humbly in His presence I bow my heart to pray.

Touch me, dear Jesus, right now, and make of me
The Christ-like person I know you want me to be.
With each trial and sorrow, please help me to gain
Compassion to comfort others in their grief and pain.

Remind me of your great love as each day begins.
That I may love as you do—enemies and friends.
Help me to grow smaller, as your light shines through.
Let there be much less of me and much more of you.

Knowing that this mortal life brings trouble and woe,
Create in me your patience; keep me close as I grow.
Fill me with your Spirit so my spirit will be sweet.
Cause your love to shine daily on each soul that I meet.

While making me your vessel to be used every day,
Remember, dear Master, that I am made of clay.
Forgive me for my failures and work I leave undone.
Renew my strength daily; my race is not yet won.

You have shown me such forgiveness, mercy and grace.
I offer up my life and my heart in grateful praise.
Cause me to always keep my eyes upon you.
Keep me faithful, humble, gentle, loving and true.

"Fellowship is sweeter, and my joy is more complete, when I kneel and pray at the Savior's feet."

GOD'S STANDARD OF JUDGMENT

If we want to find out what God's standard of judgment will be when we all stand before him, Jesus reveals that in Matthew 25:31-46. He will separate the people into two categories—the sheep and the goats. The following is just a portion of that passage:

"When the Son of Man shall come in all His glory, and all the angels with Him, then He will take His seat upon the throne of His glory...Then the King will say to those on His right hand, 'Come, you who are blessed by my Father, enter into possession of the Kingdom which has been prepared for you since the creation of the world. For I was hungry, and you gave me to eat; I was thirsty, and you gave me to drink; I was a stranger, and you gathered me in; naked, and you clothed me; I was sick, and you came to visit me; in prison, and you came to me.' Then the righteous will answer Him, 'Lord, when did we see you hungry, and nourish you? Or thirsty, and gave you to drink? When did we see you a stranger, and gather you to us? Or naked, and clothed you? When did we see you sick, or in prison, and come to you?' And the King will answer them, 'This is the truth I tell you—insomuch as you did it unto one of the least of these my brothers, you did it to me.'"

Jesus makes it very clear that one way God will judge us is by our reaction to human need. His judgment does not depend on the knowledge we have amassed, or the fame we have acquired, or the fortune we have gained, but on the help we have given. Jesus requires that we help in the simple everyday things of life that any of us can do, such as giving a hungry man a meal, a thirsty man a drink, welcoming a stranger, cheering a sick person, or visiting those who are in prison.

Jesus also points out that the help which wins the approval of God is the help which is given for nothing but the sake of giving. Those who had helped their brothers were unaware that they had helped Jesus. Helping was a natural reaction of a loving heart. There are those who will help if they are given praise and thanks and publicity; but that kind of help is for show and to bring recognition to their own selfish egos.

When we understand that we should help others in the simple things without recognition and praise being our motivation, but simply out of a loving heart, then we will truly know the joy of helping Jesus Christ Himself.

"If anyone has material possessions and sees his brother in need but has no pity on him, how can the love of God be in him? Dear children, let us not love with words or tongue but with actions and in truth." 1 John 3:17-18

SKIPPING IN
THE DARK

According to Steve Chapman in his book "A Look at Life from a Deer Stand", this is a true story told by a father to his little girl who had brought him comfort years before when he was facing a time of great testing. The verses were written by Lilah Gustafson and read at her father's funeral. It reminds fathers (and all of us) of how much our Heavenly Father cares for us.

She trembled with fear as they entered the night to shadows like shrouds o'er the land.
She whimpered, "I'm scared of the darkness ahead". He said, "Here, my child, hold my hand."
She offered hers up and she clasped it in his, her wee little fist in his palm.
The strength of his grip, and the love in his touch, to her quivering heart brought a calm.

Her fears now allayed and her courage restored, she bounced by his side with a lark.
And feeling the grasp of his hand in hers, she said, "Look! I can skip in the dark!"
Her daddy looked down at his dear little girl, so trusting, so sure of his care.
For though she could not see the path in the dark, she feared not, for Daddy was there.

The Lord sent a message through his little girl that bolstered his own troubled mind.

"I ever am with you; I'll guard every step wherever your pathway may wind.

For I am thy God, I will hold your right hand, fear not, Dear One, I will help thee,

For I am continually here by your side, still holding your hand. Trust in me."

With tears in his eyes, he looked up to the heavens; the stars gave brightness to night.

God prodded his heart, "There's no darkness on earth can ever extinguish the light.

Look up hurting child, and give me your hand, there's light on your pathway so stark.

My hold will not fail, you're secure in my grasp; you, too, child can skip in the dark."

"For I, the Lord your God, will hold your right hand, saying to you, 'Fear not, I will help you.'" Isaiah 41:13

HIS HAND IN MINE

You may ask me how I know my Lord is real.
You may doubt the things I say and doubt the way I feel.
But I know He's real today, He'll always be.
I can feel His hand in mine and that's enough for me.

I will never walk alone; He holds my hand.
He will guide each step I take,
And if I fall, I know He'll understand.
Till the day He tells me why He loves me so;

I can feel His hand in mine, that's all I need to know.
I can feel His hand in mine, that's all I need to know.

Mosie Lister

A LIFE SAVED

Years ago, when my daughter was a baby, she was in the hospital. I had spent the night by her bed, and later that morning I slipped away and went to the hospital chapel to pray. There was a young woman sitting in the chapel, and so I sat down next to her and we got acquainted. I could tell that she was probably Arabic from her accent, so I asked if she was new to America. She told me that she was and that she had come to America as a college exchange student.

As we talked, I found out that her husband was having surgery that morning and she had come to the chapel to pray for him. Then she told me the real story of how she came to be an America citizen. She told me that where she came from it was dangerous to become a Christian. Her family were Muslims. When her father and brothers found out that she had become a Christian and had a Bible, they were furious. Her mother heard them talking about how they could kill her before anyone found out what she had become.

At that time, there was a kind of secret organization that operated under the heading of a foreign exchange program. Somehow, her mother made arrangements with someone from that group to get her away from her home to freedom under the guise of becoming a college exchange student in America. She did not tell me how that was done, but they were successful in getting her here.

Once here, someone helped her get enrolled in college, and helped her get a job. She had a sponsor who helped her become a citizen. Later she got married to an American man and was living in a town nearby. Her family disowned her so she had no communication with them. She didn't know what had happened to her mother who had put her own life in danger to save her daughter.

It has been over 50 years since I met that young lady. I have often thought about her and her mother and the sacrifices they made. Even though it saved her life, it separated her from her family, friends, and home land. It is a reminder to all of us just how blessed we are to live in a country that, so far, it is still not life-threatening to be a Christian. We should pray that our nation will continue to be free from oppression and religious persecution. We should also pray for Christians who live in countries that do not have those freedoms.

"Peter said to him, 'We have left everything to follow you!' 'I tell you the truth,' Jesus replied, 'no one who has left home or brothers or sisters or mother or father or children or fields for me and the gospel will fail to receive a hundred times as much in this present age (homes, brothers, sisters, mothers, children and fields—and with them persecutions) and in the age to come eternal life.'" Mark 10:28-30

THE MASK

"Don't wear your troubles on your sleeve." "Put on a happy face." "Nobody wants to hear about your problems." You've heard these, right? True, some things in our life should be private, but we want to be accepted and loved, and it matters to us what others think about us. But it can get lonely behind some of the walls we build to protect ourselves from being hurt by life. We may sometimes feel that no one understands what we are experiencing, and that may be true. Can one person really know all about another person?

Sometimes, if we are not careful, we may even find ourselves foolishly trying to hide from God how we really feel, especially when our life seems to be out of control. We may blame God for things that happen to us that we don't understand, such as unexpected illness or tragedy in our life or the life of someone we love. It's okay to tell God you are angry with him, He already knows it, and until you talk with him, the feelings won't get resolved. You will not have peace in your heart until you do. I can offer this advice because I have been there; maybe you have too.

Do you have a mask that you wear to hide your true feelings from others or even from yourself? It's possible to wear a mask for so long that we can't remember what we looked like without it. Good news! We can take the mask off! God knows everything about us and still He loves us—warts and all, and His love gives us worth. We are a child of the

King! That is the simple, irrational truth. A few years ago, I had this truth dramatically revealed to me, and felt led to write the following words:

Only Jesus sees the real me,
The "me" that no one else can see.
He looks beyond the mask I put on.
For He alone sees the real me.

Jesus knows the way that I feel.
He can see the "me" that is real.
He looks inside where I can't hide.
For He alone sees the real me.

Jesus knows my thoughts and my heart.
He searches out my innermost parts.
He knows my fears and He draws me near,
For He alone sees the real me.

Jesus, when you search my soul, I pray
You'll find me faithful to walk in your way.
Forgive secret sins that I hide within,
For you alone see the real me.

...*"the Lord does not look at the things man looks at. Man looks at the outward appearance, but the Lord looks at the heart."* 1 Samuel 16:7

"O Lord, you have searched me and you know me. You know when I sit and when I rise; you perceive my thoughts from afar. You discern my going out and my lying down; you are familiar with all my ways." Psalm 139:1-3

"For God so loved the world that He gave His one and only Son, that whoever believes in Him shall not perish but have eternal life." John 3:16

HELLO JESUS

One day as I was leaving church, the car radio was playing a song called, "Did You Think to Pray?" It occurred to me that I had just spent two hours in God's house and not once spoken to Him personally. I had listened to others pray aloud, but had not opened up my own heart in conversation with Him. As I reflected on this, I thought about other times that I had spent a whole day and not talked to God even once. Think about it. Are you guilty of this too?

Most of us are friendly people. We speak to others with whom we come in contact, and say "Hello" to any stranger we might pass in our daily routine. When we visit in someone's home or have someone in our own home, we would never dream of spending the whole evening without speaking to them. That would be rude. We rarely go all day in our own home without talking to our family. But too often, we visit God's house without talking to Him. Shouldn't God have the same courtesy as family, friends, acquaintances and strangers. After all, he is our heavenly Father. That makes Him family.

So often in our life, we do not think to ask God for help until we realize we can't do it ourselves. We seem to think we only need to bother God with our big problems; as if we are saying to Him, "I've got this. I'll let you know if I need help." Sometimes, we should think to "bother" God with our current circumstance before we make it an even bigger problem. Many of our problems could be avoided if we would just think to ask God for guidance before we go down the wrong path. And, we should always remember to thank Him for leading us in the right way.

"Do not be anxious about anything, by prayer and petition, with thanksgiving, present your requests to God. And the peace of God, which transcends all understanding, will guard your hearts and your minds in Christ Jesus." Philippians 4:6-7

"And pray in the Spirit on all occasions with all kinds of prayers and requests." Ephesians 6:18

"Be joyful always; pray continually; give thanks in all circumstances, for this is God's will for you in Christ Jesus." I Thessalonians 5:16-18

I need to humbly pray:

When I am down and lost and just can't seem to find my way,
I must look to heaven and ask God to guide my feet that stray.
Sometimes I sin against God and I often do wrong to another.
Then, I must ask for forgiveness from God and from my brother.

When others do me harm, I must ask God to grant me grace to forgive.
Remembering His mercy covers my sins and that He died that I might live.
Often, I feel sad and lonely and need to feel the comfort of someone near.
Turning my eyes to heaven, I find Jesus never left me; He is still here.

When I need wisdom, discernment and guidance I have only to ask.
God gives what I need when I need it, to meet the challenge of His task.
Many times, God's Holy Scripture leaves me confused at what I read.
But if I ask Him for understanding, He is faithful to give me what I need.

I dare not forget and only come to God with my needs and with my wants,
And treat Him like a good fairy and expect Him to wave a magic wand.
I need to praise and thank Him whether my life is troubled or going great,
And keep a humble and thankful heart at all times, no matter what my state.

When should I pray? I need to communicate with God all day, every day.
I need to thank Him when I wake up and ask Him to lead me in His way.
As I go about my daily routine, I need to talk to Him and ever be aware
That every good thing comes from Him and that I am always in His care.

When should I pray? When my day is over and I am retiring for the night,
Asking for forgiveness for my failures and trusting Him to make them right.
I must pray for the needs of others who I may have met from day to day.
Let me be your feet, voice, and hands Lord, and let me in your presence stay.

OUR DEDICATED PASTORS

Many of our dedicated pastors became a Christian at a tender young age and answered the call to preach. While others their age may have been trying new things, like alcohol, drugs, sex, hanging out and basically doing nothing, they were studying the Bible and learning about Jesus and sharing what they learned with others.

When they decided to further their education, they could have chosen a career with good benefits, lots of time off, and a big salary. But instead, they chose a career with an uncertain salary, long hours, too much time away from their family, dealing with a lot of hard to please people, lots of moving around, and with most of the rewards to be realized after they leave this earth.

They get up before daylight and travel to an out-of-town hospital to pray with the family of someone who is undergoing major surgery. Now they could just as easily stay at home and pray, but they know that their presence is needed.

They give up their day off to perform a wedding ceremony or attend some kind of activity at the church. They could be sleeping in, playing golf, or fishing, or going to the beach? After all, that's what a lot of their congregation does some Sundays.

They forego precious time that could be spent with their own family to go and minister to the needs of someone else's family, but are still expected to raise perfect children. They are on call 24/7 just in case someone needs them.

They are often put down by the community because they don't compromise with the world's view of who they should be and who God is. They are often criticized because they are dogmatic about what the Bible teaches, and they refuse to just preach about what makes everybody feel good.

Their reputations are often smeared by disgruntled church members or by those who choose to live in sin that is not sanctioned by the Bible. They patiently sit and listen to a lot of petty and selfish complaining by the very members of their congregation who should be loving and supportive of their pastor and church.

They pray and study week after week to bring God's message to the church, and plead with the congregation to live within the will of God and come to Jesus, only to see little or no positive response.

Many of us have cried on their shoulder when life has dealt us a heavy blow; or have been overwhelmed by guilt because of some deed we have done and needed their reassurance that we are forgiven, loved and accepted. We have held their hand while standing over the final resting place of a dear loved one, and found it easier to say goodbye. We have come to realize our need for Jesus because we heard the message of the cross from a caring pastor. To these faithful pastors, we are eternally grateful and blessed to have them in our churches and our lives.

"How, then, can they call on the one they have not believed in? And how can they believe in the one of whom they have not heard? And how can they hear without someone preaching to them? And how can they preach unless they are sent? As it is written, 'How beautiful are the feet of those who bring good news.'"
Romans 10:14-15

"Let us not become weary in doing good, for at the proper time we will reap a harvest if we do not give up." Galatians 6:9

"If a church wants a better pastor, it can get one by praying for the one it has."

Reverend Robert E. Harris

GOD CAN BE TRUSTED

It's easy to trust God when things are going well. It's harder to trust God when our world begins to fall apart and we can't stop it; our enemies show up; and when tragedy strikes. Jesus wants us to have faith in Him even if we have no food and no money. The kind of faith that still trusts Him when we lose our job, family and friends desert us, and our health goes bad. Great faith sustains in storms as well as in sunshine and gives joy and peace in difficult times.

Our faith must be anchored in God, even when our circumstances don't change. He is the one that holds our world and His will must be done. We must make sure that our trust is in God and that we are trusting Him to accomplish His will, not trying to mold His will to what we want. In the Garden of Gethsemane, even as Jesus faced crucifixion, He prayed not for His own will, but for His Father's will to be done (Matthew 26:39,42,53). It's hard to follow Jesus' example, but we must try. God is faithful and can be trusted to care for his children.

"Look to the birds of the air, for they neither sow nor reap nor gather into barns; yet your heavenly Father feeds them. Are you not of more value than they?" Matthew 6:26

Jesus said in Luke 17:6, *"If you have faith as small as a mustard seed, you can say to this mulberry tree, 'be uprooted and planted in the sea, and it will obey you.'"* Oh, to have that kind of faith!

Psalm 145:17-20, tells us: *"The Lord is righteous in all His ways and loving toward all He has made. The Lord is near to all who call on Him, to all who call on Him in truth. He fulfills the desires of those who fear Him; He hears their cry and saves them. The Lord watches over all who love Him...."*

Trust God all the time. HE IS FAITHFUL.

Once I was in the path of a hurricane that raged and blew until dawn.
Suddenly there was stillness and peace and I thought the storm was gone.
But soon the storm was raging again after the eye of the storm passed thru.
Dark clouds swept across the heavens once more, covering the skies of blue.

As I reflected on this phenomenon, I thought how much it resembles my life.
God is there in the storms of my life to give me peace from trouble and strife.
But if I stray too far from Him, I find myself drowning in the cold, hard rain.
I am tossed around, bruised and afraid, caught up in doubt and sin and pain.

Then I cry out to God for mercy and strength; He is gracious to hear my prayer.
He gently draws me back to Him; forgives my sin and keeps me in His care.
When I stay close to Him in the eye of life's storms, He bids the winds to cease.
When I focus on Him and keep looking up, that's when I find joy and peace.

Thank you, God, that you have power over all the storms of my life.
Thank you, God, that you hold my hand when I have those troubles and strife.
Thank you, God, for redeeming my soul and for hearing my prayers.
Thank you, God, for your gifts of joy and peace and for keeping me in your care.

"Then he got into the boat and his disciples followed him. Without warning, a furious storm came up on the lake, so that the waves swept over the boat. But Jesus was sleeping. The disciples went and woke him, saying, 'Lord, save us! We're going to drown!'

He replied, 'You of little faith, why are you so afraid?' Then He got up and rebuked the winds and the waves, and it was completely calm. The men were amazed and asked, 'What kind of man is this? Even the winds and the waves obey him!'" Matthew 8:23-2

RECIPE FOR
CHRISTIAN LIVING

I wrote this poem, "Recipe for Christian Living", in 2003 as a preface to a cookbook my Sunday School class was publishing. I hoped to point out that just as we follow a recipe to have a cake turn out the way it should, we have a recipe for living the life that God has planned for us. It is a reminder that Christian maturity requires effort on our part, it doesn't just magically happen.

We should strive to live as God would have us live and bring Him the glory He deserves. To do so requires us to spend time daily reading His Word and spending time with him in praise and prayer. It requires us to be willing to go where He sends us and do what He asks of us. If we let His Holy Spirit guide us, we will be able to live the life that will be pleasing to Him.

Take a good measure of kindness and mix in lots of hope.
Toss in some laughter, for it's not healthy for us to mope.
Blend in some sympathy for those who need to mourn.
Add lots of forgiveness to heal relationships that are torn.

Sprinkle an unlimited amount of joy where there is sadness;
For Jesus loved to celebrate life, and we should do no less.
Stir in some wisdom and patience to keep you on the narrow path.
This will take a heap of prayer; be sure to look to heaven and ask.

To make this recipe, you will need Bible study in great amounts.
It will help you grow in grace and love and in ways that really count.
Add fellowship with other Christians to keep you strong and true;
Beat in a lot of faith and obedience, and add some friendship too.

To keep you close to the Father and in His will for you each day,
Mix in some memorized scripture to send the devil on his way.
Add some spice to taste, as this makes life sweet and fun;
Sugar to sweeten, pepper for variety, salt to preserve—we're almost done.

Because we sometimes stumble-- remember we are made of clay--
Liberally sift in the Holy Spirit, who will guide each step of the way.
Lastly, add in the most important ingredient of all, which is love.
Love holds all the rest together; it flows through you from God above.

"Anyone who lives on milk, being still an infant, is not acquainted with the teachings of righteousness. But solid food is for the mature, who by constant use have trained themselves to distinguish good from evil." Hebrews 5:13-6:1

"Do your best to present yourself to God as one approved, a workman who does not need to be ashamed and who correctly handles the word of truth." 2 Timothy 2:15

MIRACLES
FROM CRISIS

Years ago, I became ill with a large tumor that had to be surgically removed from my stomach. I was worried and scared and, like most of us, I was asking "why"? It was a long and difficult surgery that required weeks of recovery. My surgeon came to see me in the hospital. He told me that during the surgery, behind the tumor, he discovered cancer cells. He told me that if I had not had the tumor, the cancer would have spread and become undetectable. He said, "This time next year it would have been too late to save your life. Your tumor was a blessing in disguise."

Sometimes what appears to be a devastating crisis is recognized later as an opportunity for God to work a miracle. For instance, when God delivered the Israelites from Pharoah, on their journey they came to the Red Sea. They were trapped between the Red Sea in front of them and the Egyptian army behind them. God used this predicament to show His power and His glory by allowing them to cross through the water on dry land. Then, God destroyed their enemy by drowning them when they tried to pursue the Israelites by crossing the sea.

In Exodus 14:18, God said: *"The Egyptians will know that I am the Lord when I gain glory through Pharoah, his chariots and his horsemen."* In Exodus 14:31, we are told: *"And when the Israelites saw the great power the Lord displayed against the Egyptians, the people feared the Lord and put their trust in Him and in Moses, His servant."*

Think about Joseph; he was sold into slavery by his brothers as a young man and carried off to Egypt. Years later, with his willingness to be faithful to God, he became the most powerful man in the kingdom, second only to the Pharaoh. As such, God used Joseph to save Egypt and most of the known world from starvation. Joseph was able to save his own family from starvation, in spite of what his own brothers had done to him. Because of his faithfulness, the nation of Israel was able to survive.

"But Joseph said to them (his brothers), *'Don't be afraid. Am I in the place of God? You intended to harm me, but God intended it for good to accomplish what is now being done, the saving of many lives.'*" Genesis 45:5

We are surrounded by God's glory and his miracles happen every day, we just fail to recognize them. We are prone to pass them off as luck, coincidence or unexplainable. Let's pay attention and revel in the glory of God and his handiwork, and give Him the praise and honor He is due.

David wrote in Psalm 77:11-14 *"I will remember the deeds of the Lord; yes, I will remember your miracles of long ago. I will meditate on all your works and consider all your mighty deeds. Your ways, O God, are holy. What God is so great as our God? You are the God who performs miracles; you display your power among the peoples."*

LISTEN TO GOD

It is not in our nature to readily let someone else tell us what to do. We like to call the shots. Sometimes this independence goes beyond refusing to listen to other people and includes not wanting to listen to God. The Sovereign God of the universe reveals himself to all people but not everyone is willing to see. Though Jesus was God's supreme self-revelation, all the people who saw Jesus in the flesh did not see God. God always has and continues to reveal himself in many ways.

We only need to look around us to see God in His **creation**: *"For since the creation of the world God's invisible qualities—his eternal power and divine nature—have been clearly seen, being understood from what has been made, so that men are without excuse."* Romans 1:20

Sometimes God reveals Himself in **dreams and visions**: *"He (God) said, 'Listen to my words: When a prophet of the Lord is among you, I reveal myself to him in visions, I speak to him in dreams.'"* Numbers 12:6

God may choose to reveal Himself in **unusual natural phenomena**: *"There the angel of the Lord appeared to him in flames of fire from within a bush. Moses saw that though the bush was on fire it did not burn up."* Exodus 3:2

Throughout God's Word, we see how He spoke to His people through **prophets**: *"In the past God spoke to our forefathers through the prophets at many times and in various ways,"* Hebrews 1:1

He speaks to us most clearly through the Bible, His Holy **scriptures**: *"All scripture is God-breathed and is useful for teaching, rebuking, correcting and training in righteousness, so that the man of God may be thoroughly equipped for every good work."* 2 Timothy 3:16-17

God called to Job out of a storm: *"The Lord said, 'Go out and stand on the mountain in the presence of the Lord, for the Lord is about to pass by.'*

Then a great and powerful wind tore the mountains apart and shattered the rocks before the Lord, but the Lord was not in the wind. After the wind there was an earthquake, but the Lord was not in the earthquake. After the earthquake there came a fire, but the Lord was not in the fire. And after the fire came a gentle whisper. When Elijah heard it, he pulled his cloak over his face and went out and stood at the mouth of the cave. Then a voice said to him, 'What are you doing here, Elijah?'" 1 Kings 19:11-13

We read in 2 Samuel 12:1-14 that when King David was out of fellowship with God, God spoke to him through the prophet Nathan. There are many ways God can speak to us through His Holy Spirit, but we need to be listening for His voice.

The ultimate revelation of God is in His Son Jesus Christ. *"In the beginning was the Word, and the Word was with God, and the Word was God. He was with God in the beginning. Through him all things were made; without him nothing was made that has been made. In him was life, and that life was the light of men. The light shines in darkness, but the darkness has not understood it."* John 1:1-5

"The Word became flesh and made his dwelling among us. We have seen his glory, the glory of the One and Only who came from the Father, full of grace and truth." John 1:14

"..but in these last days he has spoken to us by his Son, whom he appointed heir of all things, and through whom he made the universe. The Son is the radiance of God's glory and the exact representation of his being, sustaining all things by his powerful word. After he had provided purification for sins, he sat down at the right hand of the Majesty in heaven." Hebrews 1:2-3

"Philip said, 'Lord, show us the Father and that will be enough for us.' Jesus answered: 'Don't you know me, Philip, even after I have been among you such a long time? Anyone who has seen me has seen the Father'." John 14:8-9

A personal, intimate relationship with God is the most important thing in this lifetime. It can be ours by repenting of our sins, believing that Jesus is God's Son who made the ultimate sacrifice for us, and allowing God's Holy Spirit to come and dwell in us and lead us to live in a way that will bring glory to our Heavenly Father and be pleasing to Him.

Jesus tells us in John 3:5-6: *"I tell you the truth, no one can enter the kingdom of God unless he is born of water and the Spirit. Flesh gives birth to flesh, but the Spirit gives birth to Spirit."*

"Thomas said to Him, 'Lord, we don't know where you are going, so how can we know the way?' Jesus answered, 'I am the way and the truth and the life. No one comes to the Father except through me'." John 14:5-6

AS WE MATURE
WITH AGE

"Is not wisdom found among the aged? Does not long-life bring understanding?"
Job 12:12

"Teach us to number our days aright, that we may gain a heart of wisdom."
Psalm 90:12

"If any of you lacks wisdom, he should ask God, who gives generously to all without finding fault, and it will be given unto him. But when he asks, he must believe and not doubt" James 1:5-6

Lord, thou knowest better than myself, that I am growing older, and some day will be old. Keep me from getting talkative, particularly from the fatal habit of thinking I must say something on every subject and on every occasion; and release me from the craving to try to straighten out everybody's affairs.

Keep my mind free from the recital of endless details—give me wings to get to the point. I ask for grace enough to listen to the tales of others' pains. Help me to endure them with patience. But seal my lips on my own aches and pains. They are increasing and my love of rehearsing them is becoming sweeter as the years go by.

I dare not ask for improved memory, but for a growing humility and a lessening cocksureness when my memory seems to clash with the memories of others. Teach me the glorious lesson that occasionally I may be mistaken.

Keep me reasonably sweet. I do not want to be a saint—some of them are so hard to live with—but a sour old woman (or man) is one of the crowning works of the devil. Make me thoughtful, but not moody; helpful, but not bossy. With my vast store of wisdom, it seems a pity not to use it; but thou knowest, O Lord, I want a few friends at the end.

Give me the ability to see good things in unexpected places, and talents in unexpected people. And give me, Lord, the grace to tell them so. Amen.

Anonymous

In our culture we think of youth as the good old days of life. But is it? Perhaps in God's plan, the best years of life are the last years. The tragedy is we sometimes fail to see that. Granted, some of us have physical problems that limit our activities and many of us are care- givers. But sometimes we give up too quickly; we quit; we fail to live up to our opportunities. We feel entitled to just coast through our golden years.

We try to keep our bodies healthy and fit---to do what? To feel better as we putter around the house and yard is great, but we might consider that God has allowed us the leisure of our older years to do His work. With less responsibilities—no job to go to or children to raise, we might have more time "to be about our Father's business." The point is, we may not be as old as we think we are.

There was a godly lady in a church I attended who lived to be 96 years old. She lost her hearing and could barely see, but she sent letters and cards out every week to shut-ins, people in the hospital, and anyone she heard about that needed to be remembered. It was what she was able to do, and it was not a small thing to those who received her cards. A life of Christian service opens to us the great discovery that unselfishness and joy go hand in hand. There is a task for each of us, and we need to get to it—time's a wasting!

"Let us not become weary in doing good, for at the proper time we will reap a harvest if we do not give up." Galatians 6:9

Here's a little poem by anonymous to give us a chuckle for today:

Blessed are they who understand
My faltered step and palsied hand;
Blessed are they who know my ear today
Must strain to catch the things they say.

Blessed are they who seem to know
That my eyes are dim and my wits are slow.
Blessed are they who looked away
When coffee spilled at the table today.

Blessed are they with a cheery smile
Who stop to chat for a little while.
Blessed are they who never say,
"You've told me that story twice today".

Blessed are they who know the way
To bring back memories of yesterday.
Blessed are they who make it known
That I'm loved, respected, and not alone.

Blessed are they who ease the days
On my journey Home in loving ways.

THE NARROW PATH

We have all seen Christians who, in spite of difficulties and hardships, seemed to always be upbeat, strong, and joyful. On the other hand, there are those who never seemed to get it together. They are usually worried and often seemed to be caught up in some difficult situation. We tend to attribute that to their personalities and nature. But how can Christians be so different?

Jesus tells us in Matthew 7:13-14, that one of the differences in joyful Christians and unhappy ones are the paths they have chosen to take. Sometimes Christians—especially new and immature ones—have decided to follow Jesus down the narrow path. However, they may not have been able to get off the old worldly path on which they are so comfortable because they still face the same circumstances that were there before they chose to follow Jesus. They have not yet learned to trust God and let Him have complete control over all of their life. They still want to hold back some areas of their life for themselves.

When we deny God a part of our lives, we miss some of the blessings that He has for us. He wants to be Lord of all our life all the time. If we are not careful, we will be willing to give him only the areas of our life that we feel pertain to church; but not the everyday business of living in the world. We are willing to go to church on Sunday and maybe Wednesday night; read our Bible when we think of it; and say grace and a short bedtime prayer. But we are not willing to let God influence our business deals, how we spend our money, how we treat our neighbors, how we treat our enemies, how we treat those in need, etc. Being a part-time Christian is not the way to have joy in our salvation.

It is not easy to be "prayed up" (as the old- time saints put it) all the time, but once we have chosen to take the narrow path that leads to salvation, we need to step off the old worldly path that leads in the wrong direction. If we feel like we are being pulled in two directions, it could be we are. Let's not let Satan get a foothold on our lives; let's keep our attention on Jesus and He will lead us home, and on the way, we will have that joy of our salvation.

"Enter through the narrow gate. For wide is the gate and broad is the road that leads to destruction, and many enter through it. But small is the gate and narrow the road that leads to life; and only a few find it." Matthew 7:13-14

"He will teach us his ways, so that we may walk in his paths." Micah 4:2

"I guide you in the way of wisdom and lead you along straight paths. When you walk, your steps will not be hampered; when you run, you will not stumble." Proverbs 4:11-12

"Trust in the Lord with all your heart and lean not on your own understanding; in all your ways acknowledge him and he will make your paths straight." Proverbs 3:5-6

NIGHT IS DARKEST
BEFORE THE DAWN

"Night is darkest just before the dawn". I have heard this all my life, but I never really thought much about it until I experienced it for myself. One morning while we were at our lake house, I woke up very early and decided to go out on the lake to fish. I didn't turn on any outside lights as the moon was bright enough for me to make my way to the dock and get settled into our boat. I had just backed the boat out on the lake and was preparing to head out, when the moon set.

There are no dock lights on our lake and no one was up that early to have any lights on anywhere. It was so dark that I could not see anything at all. All I could do was sit in that rocking boat and pray that I would not be buffeted into the dock. After what seemed like forever, I could see light along the eastern shore as the sun began to rise. I could see where I was going and I knew everything would be okay.

It occurred to me that life is like that at times. We go along enjoying the light and without warning everything turns dark, and we can only drift, unable to see our way. Many of us have already experienced these times, and those who haven't will experience them if they live long enough.

We are not children of darkness, but of light. In John 8:12, Jesus said, *"I am the light of the world. Whoever follows me will never walk in darkness, but will have the light of life."*

Again, in 1 John 1:5, we read, *"This is the message we have heard from Him and declare to you: 'God is light; in Him there is no darkness at all'."*

"The Lord is my light and my salvation—who shall I fear? The Lord is the stronghold of my life—of whom shall I be afraid?" Psalm 27:1

When those dark days come, turn your face toward Jesus, the "light of the world". Ask Him to lead you and then listen for His voice. His path is well-lit and leading in the right direction, so you will not lose your way. While in the dark, pray until God's light comes shining through. He is faithful.

No need to worry about the darkness; God put the sun and moon in place. He gives His children peace and joy through His precious love and grace. When troubling times come, He gives peace that He alone can supply. With His mercy and grace, He gives His children strength to get by.

Should death loom in the shadows, no need to worry about a thing. When Jesus died and rose again, He took away all of death's sting. When we reach the gates of Heaven, and His precious face at last we see. He will be there to welcome us home, for He is the one who holds the key.

LIVING ONE DAY
AT A TIME

Recently, I was driving through a neighboring town where I saw this on a church billboard: "If you are stumbling over past events, you are walking backwards." I thought how true these words can be. Sometimes it is hard to let go of what happened in the past and move forward with our life. One of life's greatest lessons I have learned is that I can only live one day at a time. We may never be able to forget our past, but we can learn to not let it define our future. With the help of God's Holy Spirit, we can move ahead and welcome each day as a gift from God.

"Moses said to God, 'Suppose I go to the Israelites and say to them, The God of your fathers has sent me to you, and they ask me: What is his name? Then what shall I tell them?' God said to Moses, 'I AM WHO I AM. This is what you are to say to the Israelites: I AM has sent me to you.' God also said to Moses, 'Say to the Israelites, The Lord, the God of your fathers—the God of Abraham, the God of Isaac and the God of Jacob—has sent me to you. This is my name forever, the name by which I am to be remembered from generation to generation.'" Exodus 3:13-15

Recently I discovered a poem that a woman, Helen Mallicoat, wrote that expressed this truth to me. She pointed out that when we are regretting things from our past or fearing what might come in the future, we should remember the name that God gave for himself. It starts out like this:

"I was regretting the past and fearing the future...

Suddenly my Lord was speaking:

'MY NAME IS I AM'."

She went on to say that living in the past is hard because God is not there; His name is not "I WAS". She points out that living in the future is hard because God is not there; His name is not "I WILL BE". Then she reminds us that when we live in the present-day, life is easier because God's name is "I AM".

"Forget the former things; do not dwell on the past." Isaiah 43:18

"Now listen, you who say, today or tomorrow we will go to this or that city, spend a year there, carry on business and make money. Why, you do not even know what will happen tomorrow." James 4:13, 14

"Therefore, do not worry about tomorrow, for tomorrow will worry about itself. Each day has enough trouble of its own." Matthew 6:34

"Therefore, God again set a certain day, calling it Today, when a long time later he spoke through David, as was said before: 'Today, if you hear his voice, do not harden your hearts.'" Hebrews 4:7

"This is the day the Lord has made; let us rejoice and be glad in it". Psalm 118:24

Of course, we know God is able to be anywhere He chooses to be—in the past, in the future, and in the present. But He does not want us to live anywhere except "today". Today is a gift from God. That is why it is called "the present".

GOD CARES ABOUT OUR SMALL PROBLEMS

I am a member of an organization that helps to provide scholarships for young women who want to pursue a college education. We take turns hosting our monthly meetings. A while back it was my turn to host the meeting and provide lunch afterwards. I carefully planned the menu of broccoli soup, chicken salad croissants, and cake for dessert.

The day of the meeting, I got a call from the club president letting me know that instead of eleven guests, I would be having sixteen, including a member of the State Board of Directors. It was too late to prepare more chicken salad for the croissants, and there was not enough time to go to a store and buy salad. I had made only twelve croissants, one for each of my eleven guests and one for myself. I was almost in tears. What was I going to do? While I was trying to come up with a solution as to what to feed my guests, my sister-in-law Shirley, a sweet Christian lady, who was helping me get everything ready, suggested that we pray over the food that I had already prepared.

She said, "If Jesus can feed 5,000 people with a child's lunch, surely, He can feed seventeen people with a bowl of chicken salad and a few croissants." We removed the salad from the twelve croissants that were already made and ready to serve. We laid our hands on the bowl of salad and prayed, asking God to provide enough chicken salad to make seventeen croissants for my guests. Our prayers were answered. We were able to make seventeen croissants with generous helpings of salad and even had salad left over.

Now, I'm sure that some people would have a lot of explanations as to how we were able to stretch the salad to meet my need. But I am convinced that God intervened and it was one of His miracles that He performs all the time; we just fail to recognize them. I believe that Jesus was trying to show me that He cares about every area of our lives. He wants to be a part of everything that matters to us. He shares our celebrations, and He shares our disappointments and problems, no matter how big or how small. If it is important to us, it is important to Him. We should not hesitate to include Him in every part of our lives and to praise Him and ask for help. He is a loving and compassionate God.

The first public miracle that Jesus performed was at a wedding party. We see from this that Jesus enjoyed having a good time with others. We see that a small detail like running out of wine was of concern to Him because it was of concern to His mother and the host of the party. We read about this in John 2:1-10.

"On the third day a wedding took place at Cana in Galilee. Jesus' mother was there, and Jesus and his disciples had also been invited to the wedding. When the wine was gone, Jesus' mother said to him, 'They have no more wine.'

'Dear woman, why do you involve me?' Jesus replied. 'My time has not yet come.'

His mother said to the servants, 'Do whatever He tells you.'

Nearby stood six stone water jars, the kind used by the Jews for ceremonial washing, each holding from twenty to thirty gallons.

Jesus said to the servants, 'Fill the jars with water'; so, they filled them to the brim.

Then He told them, 'Now draw some out and take it to the master of the banquet.'

They did so, and the master of the banquet tasted the water that had been turned into wine. He did not realize where it had come from, though the servants who had drawn the water knew. Then he called the bridegroom aside and said, 'Everyone brings out the choice wine first and then the cheaper wine after the guests have had too much to drink; but you have saved the best till now'."

HAS SATAN LIED TO YOU?

Has Satan lied to you? Some of his favorite lies are: You don't need to go to church or trust in Christ as your Savior to go to heaven. There are many ways to get to heaven; Jesus isn't the only way. You can worship God anywhere. You're a good person and do many good deeds for other. You are just as good as those hypocrites who go to church. A loving God would never let anyone perish.

It is true that there are many good people in the world who do a lot of good things for others. That just makes them good people, not necessarily Christians. It is difficult to get those good people to realize their need for Christ, especially when they see people who call themselves Christian not following Christ's teachings. Standing in a garage does not make someone a car, any more than sitting in church makes someone a Christian. Thankfully, we are not judged by what someone else does or doesn't do, but by our own actions. We are judged by whether or not we let others know about Jesus.

Romans 3:10 points out that: *"There is no one righteous, not even one."* Romans 3:20 tells us: *"Therefore, no one will be declared righteous in His sight by observing the law, rather, through the law we become conscious of sin."*

Pastor Don Walton of *Time for Truth Ministries* says it this way: "The 10 Commandments (Exodus 20:1-17) were not given to show what God is like, but to show us what we are like. God said don't and we do; God said do and we don't, leaving us guilty before God, without excuse, and knowing that we're sinners in need of a savior. God did not give us His law to get us saved, but to show us that we are lost. God gave us His Son to get us saved."

Christ came to fulfill the old covenant of the Law by giving us a new covenant of grace and redemption through His death, burial and resurrection. However, in order to be covered under this new covenant, one must accept Christ's free gift of salvation. This involves humbling ourselves and repenting of our sins and turning our life over to Christ and allowing Him to be our Master.

Thousands of years ago, the prophet Isaiah wrote: *"All of us have become like one who is unclean, and all our righteous acts are filthy rags; we all shrivel up like a leaf, and like the wind our sins sweep us away."* (Isaiah 64:6) Simply put, we just cannot do enough good deeds to be clean in God's sight. We need a mediator, Jesus Christ, to cover out sins by His precious blood that He shed on the cross, to make us acceptable in God's sight. We need a personal relationship with Christ.

Come meet my Jesus, you'll love Him right away.
He loves you; He'll walk with you from day to day.
When sorrow comes and your broken heart you can't hide;
He'll hold you in His arms; He is always by your side.

He is never too busy to listen if you want to have a talk.
And He is there to guide your steps in life's daily walk.
Come meet my Jesus, you'll love Him right away.
If you will open up your heart, He will come in to stay.

Jesus said in John 14:6: **"I am the Way and the Truth and the Life. No one comes to the Father except through me."**

GOD PROVIDES FOR HIS CHILDREN

"Then the Lord said to Moses, 'Behold, I will rain down bread from heaven for you. The people are to go out each day and gather enough for that day.'" Exodus 16:4

Then the children of Israel did as they were told; some gathered much, some little; and when they measured it by omer, he who gathered much did not have too much; and he who gathered little did not have too little. Each one gathered as much as he needed. Then Moses said to them, "No one is to keep any of it until morning." Exodus16:17-19

Significant facts about God's provision of manna for the Israelites while they were wandering for forty years in the desert, are that He always provided just enough manna for one day, and it couldn't be stored overnight. It only lasted one day before it spoiled.

This tells us that God's help is daily. Jesus must have had this thought in mind when He taught his disciples to pray, *"Give us this day our daily bread."* (Matthew 6:11) Being utterly dependent goes against the grain of our human pride; we're the kind of folks who like to captain our own ship. We tend to trust in our own ingenuity, but our God is loving and patient with us even when we push him aside. As Shakespeare once said, "What fools these mortals be." We can't even draw our next breath without God's help!

"So do not worry, saying, 'What shall we eat? Or What shall we drink? Or What shall we wear?' For the pagans run after all these things, and your heavenly Father knows that you need them. But seek first his kingdom and his righteousness, and all these things will be given to you as well. Therefore, do not worry about tomorrow, for tomorrow will worry about itself. Each day has enough trouble of its own." Matthew 6:31-34

Still, it's easy to worry, isn't it? We spend a lot of precious time with the "what ifs". In Psalm 46:1 David wrote: *"God is our refuge and our strength, a very present help in trouble."* This includes the trouble that is on our doorstep today; the trouble that kept us awake last night; the trouble that comes out of nowhere unexpectedly. God will give strength for the trouble that we face today. Why should we be occupied with what might happen tomorrow?

HIS EYE IS ON THE SPARROW

Why should I be discouraged, why should the shadows come;
Why should my heart be lonely, and long for heav'n and home;
When Jesus is my portion? My constant friend is He:
His eye is on the sparrow, and I know He watches me;
His eye is on the sparrow, and I know He watches me.

Refrain:
I sing because I'm happy; I sing because I'm free,
For His eye is on the sparrow, and I know He watches me.

"Let not your heart be troubled," His tender word I hear.
And resting on His goodness, I lose my doubts and fears.
Though by the path He leadeth, but one step I may see.
His eye is on the sparrow, and I know He watches me.;
His eye is on the sparrow, and I know He watches me.

Whenever I am tempted, whenever clouds arise,
When songs give way to sighing, when hope within me dies,

I draw the closer to Him, from care He sets me free.
His eye is on the sparrow, and I know He watches me;
His eye is on the sparrow, and I know He watches me.

Civilla D. Martin, 1905
Matthew 10:29–31

There is no situation that God cannot handle. And there is no situation you and God cannot handle together. He gives us grace to live; grace to die; grace to do all that he requires of us. You can call heaven's help line anytime, twenty-four seven, and you will never get a busy signal or voice mail. It is unproductive to live in the future, so trust our faithful God to give you grace for living today.

GIVE YOUR
BEST TO GOD

My good friend and I were discussing the importance of giving. In the course of this discussion, she told me how this lesson was impressed upon her as a teenager. When her father became a Christian, he truly became a new creature. Up until that time he was worldly in every sense of the word. He made up for the lost years with his generosity and his faithfulness to Christ. She told me that if she had never heard a sermon, she would believe in Christ because of the extraordinary change she witnessed in her father.

One day her father came home and told her and her sister that there was a family in need of clothing. He told them to go to their closet and find some clothing to give to this family. They looked through their clothes and pulled out the oldest ones and the ones they didn't particularly like to wear. They brought these to their father. He looked them over and asked, "These are old clothes you don't wear any more, aren't they?" They had to admit that they were.

Her father told them to go back to their closet and get their very best clothes to give to the family in need. She said, "We got a Bible lesson on how we should give our very best to God because we had been so blessed by Him. At the time, we were not so happy about doing that. But, over my lifetime, I have come to better understand what my daddy was trying to teach me."

Some people question whether tithing is taught in the New Testament. In his book, "It's a God Thing", noted ministry evangelist Dr. Charles Roesel, tells us that tithing is reaffirmed by Jesus in the gospel of Matthew.

"Woe to you, teachers of the law and Pharisees, you hypocrites! You give a tenth of your spices—mint, dill and cumin. But you have neglected the more important matters of the law—justice, mercy and faithfulness. You should have practiced the latter, without neglecting the former. Matthew 23:23

In other words, you should tithe, but don't think that by tithing you can pay God off. How you live is just as important as how you give. Some Christians point out that this scripture is the only place where the Lord endorsed tithing, along with the parallel passage in Luke 11:42. This suggests to them that the New Testament presents a weak case for tithing.

My question is, 'How many times does Jesus have to say something before we believe it?' There is another passage mentioned by Jesus only one time. Jesus said in John 3:7, *'You must be born again.'* Obviously, this is an important truth! John 3:7 is central to the gospel of Jesus Christ. We preach it and teach it. In regard to tithing, Jesus affirms it only once in God's Word. It is no less a weighty truth. Our Lord made no idle comments."

In 2 Corinthians 9:11, Paul tells us this: *"You will be made rich in every way so that you can be generous on every occasion, and through us your generosity will result in thanksgiving to God."* God gave us the very best He had in His son Jesus. We can do no less that give Him back our first fruits and the very best we have of that with which He has so richly blessed us.

FLOYD'S WEDDING RING

A few years ago, my husband Floyd and I were at our home on a lake. One day we decided to clean out a flower bed and plant some azaleas. By mid-afternoon we had filled up three large lawn bags with leaves and roots from the flower bed. Floyd was washing his hands when he discovered his wedding band was missing. The band was gold with five diamonds, and it was one of his most prized possessions.

We immediately began looking for the ring. We searched the flower bed inch for inch but could not find the ring. We dumped out the lawn bags and went through the debris with our bare hands but there was no sign of the ring. We decided that we might be able to find it with a metal detector. So, we drove for a couple of hours back to our home in town to get a metal detector.

The next morning, we drove back to the lake. We went over the whole flower bed with the metal detector, as well as the debris we had dumped out and searched the day before. We decided to take a water break and then go over everything again. I could tell that Floyd was devastated that we were not able to find his ring.

I went into the house and knelt down on the living room floor and prayed: "God, Floyd has lost his wedding ring and you know how much it means to him. I know that a ring is not so important when you weigh it against other things going on in our world, but he is so sad and dejected that it breaks my heart to see him like that. If you do not help us, we will not find his ring. Please help us. Thank you, Father."

After a few minutes, I went back outside to continue the search. I looked down into the flower bed, and there was the ring, in plain sight on top of the ground where we had already searched several times. It looked like someone had just put it there; it wasn't even dirty. I looked around, half expecting to see an angel. I remember thinking, "Why didn't I ask God to help us yesterday? We wasted a lot of time and effort doing it alone."

I have told this story to a lot of people and have heard a lot of opinions on how it turned out. I am still amazed that so many people do not believe in miracles. Some have said it was a coincidence that we found the ring so easily after praying. Others have told me how lucky we were to find the ring. Others said we just overlooked it. But I know that we found it because God, in His great love and compassion, answered my prayer. I was reminded of a great truth that day. I had forgotten that God is concerned with our everyday activities and problems, and that **we should always seek His will and guidance first in every situation**.

"Therefore, whatever you ask for in prayer, believe that you have received it, and it will be yours." Mark 11:24

"Ask and it will be given to you, seek and you will find; knock and the door will be opened to you. For everyone who asks receives; he who seeks finds; and to him who knocks, the door will be opened." Matthew 7:7–8

YOU REAP WHAT YOU SOW

Daddy was a raised on a farm. Whenever we lived where it was possible to have a garden, he would plant one. He told about an incident that happened to him and his brothers when they were young boys. Perhaps this story applies to you, or you know someone who has done something like this. Daddy and his brothers were given the task of planting a row of corn in the family garden. But, being boys, they were much more interested in going fishing in a nearby pond than they were in planting corn.

They started out planting the kernels as close together as they had been taught to do. But as time went by, they began to plant them further and further apart. When they got to the end of the row, they still had a lot of kernels left. Rather than go back and replant the row, they decided to just dig a hole behind the barn and throw the remainder of the kernels in the hole so they could get on down to the pond sooner.

Well, you know what happened. The corn began to come up with so much distance between each plant that Grandpa got suspicious about how it had been planted. The thing that really sealed their fate was the corn that came up in one big clump behind the barn.

In this life, as Christians, the Bible warns us that we should be careful about what we sow and how we sow. If what we do is done out of pride and selfishness, we will reap destruction; but if our actions are done to please God, we will reap eternal life.

"As I have observed, those who plow evil and those who sow trouble reap it. At the breath of God, they are destroyed; at the blast of his anger, they perish." Job 4:8-9

"Do not be deceived: God cannot be mocked. A man reaps what he sows. The one who sows to please his sinful nature, from that nature will reap destruction; the one who sows to please the Spirit, from the Spirit will reap eternal life." Galatians 6:7-8

It seems that sometimes what we sow does not yield a harvest; but we must remember that some of our harvest will not be reaped here in this life. But some of what we sow may go ahead of us to heaven or be realized here on earth after we are gone.

My mother-in-law was the most-saintly Christian that I ever knew. She had a child-like faith in Jesus that was unshakeable; she could always see the good in everyone and she believed that everything that came into her life would somehow be a blessing. She truly demonstrated that in her life, God was in charge. I remember her saying that she prayed every day for her family. Her constant prayer was that each of her seven children would come to know Jesus during their lifetime. After she was gone to be with the Lord, her prayer was answered, even though she was not here to see it come to pass.

"Let us not become weary in doing good, for at the proper time we will reap a harvest if we do not give up." Galatians 6:9

LIFE GOES ON

Have you ever had times in your life that you felt just too tired of everything to go on? Those are the times when life keeps knocking you down, and before you can get back on your feet again it gives you another blow. How often do you deal with feelings that "life stinks"? How easily we can jump from "life stinks" to "God isn't there". You are discouraged, tired, and may even begin to have doubts about God's love; does He really care, and if so, where is He and why can't I feel his presence? After all, He is in charge of everything. Many of us have been there and it is not a happy place.

Psalm 145:13-20, tells us: *"Your kingdom is an everlasting kingdom, and your dominion endures through all generations. The Lord is faithful to all His promises, and loving to all He has made. The Lord upholds all those who fall and lifts up all who are bowed down. The eyes of all look to you, and you give them their food at the proper time. You open your hand and satisfy the desires of every living thing.*

The Lord is righteous in all His ways and loving toward all He has made. The Lord is near to all who call on Him, to all who call on Him in truth. He fulfills the desires of those who fear Him; He hears their cry and saves them. The Lord watches over all who love Him."

A few years ago, our family suffered some devastating illnesses almost simultaneously. It was a dark time for us and there seemed to be no end to the pain and suffering. During this time, I learned some important truths about the love and compassion of our God, and I felt lead to write the following words. I hope they will speak to your heart.

My life was in shambles, my spirit was so low;
There was no peace in my heart, where could I go?
I heard the voice of Jesus calling so sweet,
"Come to me, precious one. Lay your cares at my feet."

The world had overtaken me; I was flanked on all sides.
But the Master is faithful, His love still abides.
From the Beginning, my Lord had a plan
To love me; to save me; to keep me in His hand.

"Come to me, precious one. Lay your cares at my feet.
I will give eternal life and a joy that is complete.
I will carry your burdens and give you sweet rest.
In my arms you'll be safe, and forever be blest."

With my doubt and my pain, I made my way to the cross,
To the feet of Jesus.

Jesus said in Matthew 11:28 *"Come to me, all you who are weary and burdened, and I will give you rest."*

"Is any of you in trouble? He should pray." James 5:13

"The righteous cry out, and the Lord hears them; He delivers them from all their troubles. The Lord is close to the brokenhearted and saves those who are crushed in spirit. A righteous man may have many troubles, but the Lord delivers him from them all." Psalm 34:17-19

God does not leave us. He provides strength to endure, which produces spiritual and moral character. The daily adversities and difficulties we face because we serve Him can strengthen our faith. They can cause us to depend more on Jesus and be drawn closer to Him.

"Praise be to God and Father of our Lord Jesus Christ, the Father of compassion and the God of all comfort, who comforts us in all our troubles, so that we can comfort those in any trouble with the comfort we ourselves have received from God." 2 Corinthians 1:3-4

"He who dwells in the shelter of the Most High will rest in the shadow of the Almighty. I will say of the Lord, 'He is my refuge and my fortress, my God, in whom I trust.'" Psalm 91:1-2

"In this world you will have trouble. But take heart! I have overcome the world." John 16:33

LET'S NOT BE GRUDGE HOLDERS

In Luke 15:11-31, Jesus tells a story of what has become known as *The Parable of the Prodigal Son.* I have heard many sermons about the prodigal son. Once I heard a preacher ask if we could tell the main difference between the son who left home and the one who stayed behind. I thought of a lot of differences that he might have been referring to, but what he wanted us to see is that both of the sons were in a pigsty, but only the younger son realized it. Whenever we judge the behavior of another, it is a wise thing for us to take a look around and see if we have any mud on us.

The first step to forgiveness from our Heavenly Father is to realize that we too are sinners and that we need to repent of our sins. We cannot earn the forgiveness of Jesus—it is free to those who confess their sins to him and ask for his mercy. But we must remember that in order for us to be forgiven we must be willing to forgive those who wrong us. The words of Jesus in Matthew 6:14 tells us: *"For if you forgive men when they sin against you, your heavenly father will also forgive you. But, if you do not forgive men their sins, your father will not forgive you."* What a sobering thought!

Sometime forgiving someone who has wronged us is very difficult—almost impossible to do. It may be a gradual process and it may take time, but with the help of the Holy Spirit it can be done. We may think we have forgiven them, but then something happens to bring back the hurt and bitterness. Then the process has to begin again. Sometimes we have to forgive someone who doesn't even know that they have wronged us. If we went to them and said, "I forgive you for what you did", they would not even know what we were talking about.

It is especially hard to forgive those who have wronged us and show no regret for their actions, realizing they would probably do it again if given the chance. It doesn't mean that what they did doesn't matter. Remember, they are accountable to God for their actions and it is not our responsibility to execute judgment—that's God's job and we need to leave that to Him.

Holding a grudge against someone means that person is in control of your feelings. Forgiving is not an option if we are to experience true peace and freedom in our Christian life. And, usually, it is impossible to do without God's help. As Christians, we have been forgiven so much that we cheapen the unfathomable forgiveness of Jesus when we hold a grudge against another. When we really understand how much God has forgiven us, it is easier to overlook the faults of others.

"Bear with each other and forgive whatever grievances you may have against one another. Forgive as the Lord forgave you. And over all these virtues put on love, which binds them all together in perfect unity." Colossians 3:13-14

A "CHRIST" CHRISTMAS

It may not be Christmas now, but it never hurts to take a minute and ponder the amazing story of how the Holy God of heaven lowered himself to become a man in a sinful world to bring salvation to you and me. It is truly something to be remembered all the time.

A few years ago, I was doing my annual last minute Christmas shopping in a local department store. As usual, crowds of people were busily checking out the bargains and hurrying to get finished with their shopping. As I walked around the store, it occurred to me that in all the trappings and decorations for the season, there was nothing to indicate what Christmas is all about.

There were snowmen, Santa Claus, gaily decorated Christmas trees, ornaments, etc. displayed all over the store. But there was no manger scene, Wise Men, Christmas star, or anything I could see that represented the birth of Jesus Christ. I thought how sad that so many had either forgotten or didn't even know why Christmas is celebrated.

I could hear music in the background. The song "I'm Dreaming of a White Christmas" could be heard all over the store. It is a beautiful song that we hear every Christmas season. Along with my apology to Irving Berlin who wrote that song, I offer my version of that song.

I'M DREAMING OF A "CHRIST" CHRISTMAS

I'm dreaming of a "Christ" Christmas, just like the ones that we should know.
Where we know the reason that we honor the season
That is more than trim and mistletoe.

I'm dreaming of a "Christ" Christmas, one that is more than Christmas trees.
Where each man is a brother, where we love one another,
Where we all can live in perfect peace.

I'm dreaming of a "Christ" Christmas, where we remember Christ who came,
To bring peace on earth through His Holy birth
And redeem those who call upon His name.

I'm dreaming of a "Christ" Christmas, one where we take some time to pause.
These busy days may we think of something more,
And remember Christmas is more than Santa Claus.

"But the angel said to her, 'Do not be afraid, Mary, you have found favor with God. You will be with child and give birth to a son, and you are to give him the name Jesus. He will be called the Son of the Most High. The Lord God will give him the throne of his father David, and He will reign over the house of Jacob forever, his kingdom will never end'." Luke 1:30-33

"But the angel said to them, "Do not be afraid. I bring you good news of great joy that will be to all the people. Today in the town of David a Savior has been born to you, he is Christ the Lord." Luke 2:10-11

THE PARABLE OF
THE SOWER

When Jesus talked with His followers, many times He told them parables to teach them a message of truth. In Matthew 13:1-9 we read the Parable of the Sower. It teaches us the reality of what we can expect when we share the gospel with the world. It reminds us that we are charged with the task of sharing God's plan of salvation with others. We sow the seed and God will help it grow and He will reap the harvest.

Few things are more discouraging than to try to share the gospel with someone who is unwilling to listen. We all have friends and family who have bought into the worldly "isms" and who somehow see us as relics of the past. When we face such opposition, sometimes the only course of action is setting a good example and prayer, lots of "from the heart" prayer. Remember, even Jesus was unable to win over everyone He spoke to about the Kingdom of God. But, His last words on earth were for us to preach His message to all people. It was important enough for Him to die on a cross, so it should be important to us.

A farmer went out to plant his field one warm and sunny day.
Birds quickly devoured some of the seed that fell along the way.
Some sprang up but soon withered as they fell on stony ground.
Some grew but were soon choked out by the thorns that had them bound.

Others fell on fertile soil as the farmer planted his field.
These seeds sprouted, grew and matured, and gave a fruitful yield.
The Master told this story long ago to crowds that gathered near.
When we understand its message, we can witness without fear.

Don't worry how others react when you sow the seeds of God's Word.
Jesus tells us there are different ways His message may be heard.
Some will hear but not understand as Satan steals it from their heart.
As shown by seeds falling by the wayside that never got a start.

Some respond quickly but when troubles come, they cannot be found.
They have no roots to sustain them, like seeds falling on stony ground.
Some understand the gospel message but the words they heard are lost.
They give time and talent to worldly things—not willing to pay the cost.

But thanks be to God, some hear and accept and bear fruit manyfold.
They are like seeds that fall on good soil, with roots that go deep and hold.
Jesus told this parable to show how His Word might be received;
So that we can understand the way His message might be perceived.

Let's look into our hearts and reflect on this message from our Lord.
Which seed shows in your life? Are you deeply rooted in God's Word?
Are you like the seeds that fell by the wayside or on stony ground?
Do you bear fruit or do the weeds of the world have you tightly bound?

Years have come and gone since Jesus told this story by the sea.
But there's still a message in it, and it's important to you and me.
Even though we may not see the harvest from the seeds that we sow,
Let's keep planting seeds and trust God to water and help the seeds to grow.

ROMAN ROAD
TO SALVATION

If you do not know my Jesus personally, these scriptures from the book of Romans in the Bible will guide you on the path to becoming a Christian. Read and study them, and if you have questions, talk to someone who is a Christian to get help in making the most important decision you will ever make.

If you are already a Christian and you want to witness to a person who is not, an effective way to do that is to use scripture verses from chapters 3 through 10 of the Book of Romans. This has become known as the *Roman Road to Salvation*. These chapters in Romans teach a clear and easy way to understand how to become a Christian. It is often used by lay people to lead someone to Jesus.

Romans 3:23: *"For all have sinned and fallen short of the glory of God...."*

Romans 6:23: *"For the wages of sin is death, but the gift of God is eternal life in Christ Jesus our Lord."*

Romans 5:8: *"But God demonstrates his own love for us in this: While we were still sinners, Christ died for us."*

Romans 10:9-10: *"That if you confess with your mouth, 'Jesus is Lord', and believe in your heart that God raised him from the dead, you will be saved. For* it is with your heart that you believe and are justified, and it is with your mouth that you confess and are saved."

Romans 10:13: "Everyone who calls on the name of the Lord will be saved."

Once, someone showed me how to remember the order of these Bible verses when we are talking to someone about how to become a Christian. First, make sure you know Romans 3:23, and start there. In your Bible next to Romans 3:23, write Romans 6:23. Next to Romans 6:23, write Romans 5:8, and at that verse write Romans 10:9-10. Then at Romans 10:9-10, write Romans 10:13. In this way, you will be able to readily turn in your Bible to the next verse in the series, as you witness to someone.

YOU MUST BE BORN AGAIN:

"...and Jesus declared, 'I tell you the truth, no one can see the kingdom of God unless he is born again.' 'How can a man be born again when he is old?' Nicodemus asked. 'Surely he cannot enter a second time into his mother's womb!'

Jesus answered, 'I tell you the truth, no one can enter the kingdom of God unless he is born of water and the Spirit. Flesh gives birth to flesh, but the Spirit gives birth to spirit.'" John 3:3-4

THE GREAT COMMISSION:

"Then the eleven disciples went to Galilee, to the mountain where Jesus told them to go. When they saw him, they worshiped him, but some doubted. Then Jesus came to them and said, 'All authority in heaven and on earth has been given to me. Therefore, go and make disciples of all nations, baptizing them in the name of the Father and of the Son and of the Holy Spirit, and teaching them to obey everything I have commanded you. And, surely, I am with you always, to the very end of the age'." Matthew 28:16-20

John tells us in Revelation 22:20-21: "He who testifies to these things says, **'Yes, I am coming soon.'** Amen. Come, Lord Jesus. The grace of the Lord Jesus be with God's people. Amen"

Printed in the United States
by Baker & Taylor Publisher Services